T0151057

My first painting
will be "The Accuser"

PHILIP JENKS

ZEPHYR PRESS
2005

Cover art is a detail from the painting "The Lion Hunter"
        by Elizabeth Jenks
Book design by *typeslowly*
Text set in Adobe Caslon and Minion
Printed in Michigan by Cushing-Malloy

Zephyr Press acknowledges with gratitude the financial support
of the National Endowment for the Arts and the Massachusetts
Cultural Council.

**NATIONAL
ENDOWMENT
FOR THE ARTS**

MASSACHUSETTS CULTURAL COUNCIL

Library of Congress Cataloging-in-Publication Data

Jenks, Philip, 1967-
  My first painting will be "The accuser" / Philip Jenks.-- 1st ed.
      p. cm.
   ISBN 0-9761612-0-6 (alk. paper)
   I. Title.
   PS3610.E55M9 2005
   811'.6--dc22

                                  2005000847

09 08 07 06 05   98765432 first edition

ZEPHYR PRESS
50 Kenwood Street
Brookline, MA 02446
www.zephyrpress.org

Acknowledgments

Some poems in this collection were first published in the following journals and magazines:

"Witch" and "mess violet": *Chicago Review*. Spring, 2005.

"Skittish outside the whisper": *FO A RM*. Magazine No. 3. Duals and Doubles. Fall, 2004.

"Hydra 1 and 2" (from the Hydra Series): *The Poker*. Premier Issue. Winter, 2003.

"Not the eyehole or looking" and "First There Was No Sun" *The Gig*. 15: Winter edition.

"Fugitive" and "Heart, Old Sop": *Monkey Puzzle*. 1. Seattle. 2002.

"Daughter": *Cultural Society Miniside No. 2*. Design/Layout by Sargasso Group. Production by Lunalux. Limited Editions. December, 2001.

"Shipwrecked, I guess," "Who the Burn Marks," "Ligature and Commence," "Boat and Fiery Circle Above," "There with the Promise Allowed," "My Eyes are Two Blank Tasks," Selections from "The Hydra Series": *The Cultural Society*. Edited by Zachary Barocas. www.culturalsociety.org. 2001-2003.

Additional Credits

"Witch" appears on *Neil Michael Hagerty and the Howling Hex*. DC227. LP. Chicago: Drag City. 2003.

"My First Painting" modifies one line from "Manimal," The Germs. *What We Do Is Secret*. LP. Los Angeles: Slash Records. 1981.

Contents

"What's left after what one isn't is taken away is what one is."
(Diane Arbus 1959 Notebook (No. 1) *Revelations*. New York:
Random House, 2003. p. 264.)

★★★

ligature and commence
ballast or last dance
my own, my little, hand
corrupts the air I walk in again.
even the head is imperfect
keeps "no time." not the way
ice melts or jutting outward
the dim profile of you
are my horizon.

★★★

Boat and fiery circle above
runnied in ditch — love has
its way with leaves, torpor.
Look at the legs, casted
from the helm through
tiny telescopes and report nothing.

Everything burns down the
heads turn talking to paper;
Cuts a raft loose from its origin,
red eyed coots blackened
bleat and cough closer to land
w/webbed green feet and some
sweet motion of severance.

★★★

a disenchanted ody was the wings
who would sign from the ribs
of a carrier pigeon? i wanted to
see you from and also prior to
what is departed. cleft of overpass
or sick to the sideways animal
kingdom. over a sprawl of coffee
table and crumb carpet bombing
histories.

★★★

i lived inside of you
and there was more
a nodding parallel
sifted splitting in
mauve regress
"shines the rain"

you produced me
you glazed
eyees with measure
or chalice. they look
themselves they look
and was timed by a
tiny hook which hung
a fan ceiling plattered
a baptist at every post.

radiator and fan
starpost and atlas
do all you can
with a whip and
a measure of malice.

★★★

maybe in a little bit.
a box for the future
hung after what will be.
Th here street will be was
stopped or checkt clikt
hung spiders from sprung
toadstools
root and dagger, a bit to chew on
clencht for you prophet,
9 do you have your maybe too?

part articles n stolid
paper days news of the news

legwork in median
peripatal retina.

★★★

my eyes are two blank tasks
filling unfilling with bent crows
and the temperature of trains
"this should be enough"
again and again in rows
the eyes are connected to the brains
and a mute forehead
hangs in universe
or mouse — an iris
can flatter or demure.

Years are born of this
the two
cross-sectioned laterally
by stretches of redwood
reversing mortal routines
I came after you
tell the west and watch
the engines blow
the mind no match
for utterance or snow.

★★★

there with the promise   allowed
frequented in urine folded fluorescence
behind the heft of plaid pantry
it's unforgettable arm in wall slumber
and Pela spins he says it's high time
and time is of essence; he humps
holes into the cataphract of degrees and cigarette protect us.

directly cross-sectioned through the doors of the store
through and wild adhesions alabastered
hummed and reticent with the courage of listing
its own listening, through even your cameras
3.75 marlboros   halfcase   skoal
and lottery through that venison you car
left with it and you make change even;
so it's retinal and lucid in every way you speak.
star and earthbound iridescent He falls apart
off his bones in the aisle and is a wander
plus a satyr hs vicious logos and legions
of blueprints)

Hydra I

have not received the new book of Apparitions
cruciferae six stamen salad
her garibaldi orange hover over
in dressing in orange six springs
spell the 30,000 of it
spelled by pectoral and upward glance
or adrift me finger the piano

forks thy father's name   (stamen and pedal)
stippled w/the phenomenal no matter
but its own flux
this tweeter is a jewel box of turmeric
jeweled in turmeric ruddy flung fiasco
enumerated w/countenance brown old growth built
cabin and heave of flung shed shattered shed
go on down yank the plates in spur

let the war yao the governor "*no native dignity warned him*
against the preposterousness
of making himself the prophet of a woman" (Arendt 1933)

ß

Promerops a mouthful of bees
the 50,000 begun gun sackled the Pelagians;
apartment ruminates Governor Pela's last stand
spent an runnied so's as to spineless
shastered sputtied and that's one wide
sally forth in lung puddles breathing in he heckles

"I leave no Will — God and vomit share a letter."
He is president of a doorway
The Real built in shackles
Whore spit and gutter
"Accursed be the soil because of you.
With suffering shall you get your food from it" (G3: 19–20).
May is the month of money and shit
He hep w/all these towers
He reverses all the verses
And make the vertical into hearses.

I, I'm wrapped in handles so as to demonstrate
this loose cause cannoned or shackled
try to triple him cast out consequence
long coffees and hippie bands
fins of foam ruppy and consequentially condensed

piano make but a frinkle like a hiccup or a nickel
I play so as to Hail in all and all is given
splintered and riven sweet nothing
to rail about in split circles
cast the widest net w/bowls of bible tripe.

(write a poem precisely in this form all over again.)
my ring my fucking ring i want my fucking ring god damn it
it is my fuck dsai she h sh to she took my ring i keep the battlefield
with my pocketwatch and address list
Next to the head fitted with paper mache treaties

Upheld and fostered February draped in snow muted leaves
Stuffed with eyes "vengeance to my God is killing me"

Slittered the net yanked its consequence
Shattered the voice crankled. Slip through to the Third Way
Split-side and suppered
Baptized beyond belief so it's not vertical
But fed my Third Side sideways sprung forth in fire
And spoke
For every four it will multiply
"Zeebedee," "boat." (Matt 3:9–4:22)
Again on the Second day,
A snapping field w/out the vertical
Sings in multiples what talks to you sideways?
Nothing forever sever lamposts I'm
Lying sideways looking in tentacles
Or rapping unmounted in airwaves
It's illustrious to shackle w/mandible
Air is of sap and and all that is acute clausterphobes
In airy open rain veils rocks and sandals

Wander up and talking unattached
Flaming, destiny with a whip
Dousing, and another way
A way tho is neither
And fossils the nor
Hydra Held.

When it's not my fault
When sullied sluice of hymn
When remnant and the visitor
When coordinate and rubric
Ascends limp and faltered
By dawn's blue brutality

Hydra II–V

hydra II

a grassy room without vegetables
and is where to sing amazing graves
or is navigable — hair carpets
her vast collection of collectibles.

dust settles everything
what you gather is predetermined
by these activities I/thee
reproached in ridiculous vacuum.

II. (

smear a painting out of it
hot gas lines exhume
everything joe mccarthy
said or did i can replace it
alphabetically every fixture
filled with camera canisters

and "loosed upon" what you
will not talk. bill madlock
exemplified this before his
buttons were pushed. bill
madlock is a a screen for the
possibility of going mad,
even as a coach.

which is the lighted side of leaves,
which turns over and glowers
which is why you're graded
and explains the inception
of filmed court proceedings.

flowers go mad and are filmed by no one.

III.

what they did made sense at the time.
to think about this

MOVE was very popular for
a philadelphia moment)
which is central to the organizing
principle, which turns on —
"part of a century"
"Pagoda" and high rise
feral.

IV.

when you was in tune
all the animals who lived
in your room. i believe in
witches should not have hung,
which

V.

where is everything.
in its context,
speaks the "disappeared"
where cuts through
is the lived parceled
composite regnant
an inhabitant
I'm an animal
with grey green horizons

that the ridges of branches
perceptibly be
where the animals live
untold or free,

whole dialects stricken
where it becomes "town"
the silence is coming.

★★★

Shipwrecked, I guess or
about to come in.
This, I understood — a landing
its consequence map muted …
Epipelagic movement enfolds
one thousand giant clams
thriving on the ocean floor.
"the field."   its reciprocity.

***

ballad of a horizon
you go to the shovel
and love and dig
up cana's body
'go to the earth and empy'
usually, the corpose
is reverse inhysterated
jellyfish for eyes and
flesht in hands in columns.
you a monster
but the shins
are wiretapped rudimentary
impulse catastrophe
for binges of ruddy and tongues
pulled open for wedding tabs.

***

I found unkempered
Witless or plant consciousness
Two stories of wisteria
Krakt paint chips
Slung cellar door
And window face
Pane winds or
Grapple sometime a castle.

★★★

city country and ?
Aphasia: no more classes.
A hymn stuck in the clavicle —
Birth, butchery and imagination
Which is both sung and ript free
In yr. History of "time's body."
This, how we talk
And that, the deadpost w/wind all around it
(is also adhesion)

★★★

Inhysterated old habits have a sheen
Bridges underhood this w/captains
And charlatan panting
We hit land once
What's a field?
It's recompense and your compassionate
Blood sockets.

★★★

The rice protein symphony
slit for mingle in the docile
"all at once," and so — directed.

it's a cough haven,
the way sojourn would be
mortified in concert with his
very own lunging owl.

★★★

Skittish outside the whisper
What you almost herde
When you was born
or were in Orcas Island
transmit bekommen a cross
meridian to heliotrope
turned —

body double buried risen
moment you bled into the world
placenta and all. Cede the placenta
to placate your form
now rising

nothing went away
when you were
and came back when
you weren't

mother was coughing
and nothing was in
the rasp
poor nothing
emptied of everything
or turns at twilight
engorged glorious
void outside the anvil
shadows no pretense
and beautiful nothing
has nothing to fret about.

Flit crane wing
Air between the span
Cant even approach
This simple rule
Where nothing is happening

Witch

A life that wasn't was —
saw it in half, sewn to scribble.
Tried in halves with working wings,
Angelic — no King or Queen to stand
but saluted randomly,
by particle, by mist
and distributed.
Blesséd be you
that which hides nothing
in your hiding.

★★★

Bell or containment
What is skin
Does or cellular despair

Where we were kept
 And made to sing for hymn
Was one of us.

An eye dissected on a pan
Fish still moving

The virgin mary in labor
Was named Mary.
What happened to the placenta?

The young woman prophesied
The death of Mary while giving birth
And we were to find she was a fish
Among many we underwater had to find her
Scraggled or listen to the water she was in
To find and found a boy so eager that he pushed
The fish downward and killed her.
Was the young woman a prophet or conspirator?
At this moment, upon pushing the water disappeared
Rattlesnake and alligator reptilian found it in a leaf,
Was bitten and forgotten by you.

———

rigid artifice what is old?
"Two years ago where did I turn?"
16?

"when I woke up I was in my bed
....no not at all but I must have"
"apparently I ended up at Susie's"

-le
lust fuckers every one trusts each other
momentarily.
Over here, hello snake I sold the bible
in my afterbirth.
Not another but not a lover, most.
Sometimes it's common practice to be minimum wage....or
lower pay less"
Walk silently with care in white shoes
20 dollar change of program or whatever the fuck that means
45?
Ahhh jeez
Then I had a hysterectomy
"Even when it's a good thing it's a "bad" thing"
Even the Accreditation company understands

Laugh and sneeze, cough lightly
Bird "youre right there south … south….

Y 7 lanes to get here san diego.
My shirt reads "DON'T STOP TOUCHING ME"
From a silkscreen of stopsign
Am I still the same student?
"you know you walked past us in the parking structure"
"yes, I did."

The sign is in north Portland.

1050 miles to this seat.

I can go find it
___

Mary died giving birth but the fish lived for a spell before an
aspect of hell.
Light lighted forced birth ws fukt in crevice
Or mayh autogenesis fifty alarm clocks timed one minute
each apart from the other to arrive this land is our land (
but there was a hot desert)

heredity flickering eyeholes lived life versus

(I'm sorry that your veteran husband died in viet nam before
you came here and that you and your 8 yr old daughter were
held hostage at gunpoint. I am. I know she told you after he
took everything she said it's ok mom we have each other we
have what matters.)

do te fishe have a kenowledege ofe thise?

"I read a book about violence in the Carolinas remind me to
never go there this guy he said that w/out recognizing that
masculinity and violence are related in a few other places
too.......they is guarding dope fields. And this the king and
that the palace no difference would you incorporate your
enemy, cannibalize as if this were a distinction too.

A catholic man named butch who says he's a cowboy calls
me when I woke up there was a german who had lived in
Oklahoma with Algonquins for 3 years prior in my room.

Hydra fucks

In the bedroom — where such a bedroom be
Binds the soul, flung him at what was the light
Breathed out his eyes done an open
Cross thickets of buildings little animal
Born under porch corners
Is also breathing
Me and possum were there to take each
Others' air. Microscopic beads
An Hydra is the corner
And the light that makes it
Breathes itself into aether eternal
Tether and antler more a matter
Of distributing the scatter
Draw a jigsaw out of it.

Thankful for the thicket
Is grabbed by what came out of it
Eye makes the seen and lungs
A camera into visceral mechanic chimera.

★★★

Is not not nothing
State unfurls its foamy mast
hide
Cross-hatched reptiles
Who slowly motion
To one another
So you peak to me
In peeled skin
Words is yr cover
And you is not
My brother

Electric leopard skinned
Smokers eating veal
With barbarous husks
Of blacktop backdrop
Down pass 23red an alder
Poleees use me to make furniture
Alder to cultostomer
      Imagine a building
      Made of your family's teeth
How many animal in your
Burger Kingdom?
Steps into eating street
With a row of mouths behind
Hydra say shh walk this way....

for H.F.

1.

Mess violet coiled
rings
Errinerung
Remember memento
Meant and unmeant meanings
Serpent trapeze.
Sea salt.
Turns orange to bright blue
Sky or the insides
Bones ps, Bladder cabinets —
"Master of the Life of Mary"
(the art lovers' cabinet)

2.

blast Master written
on wrists a permanent
Mark. Being IBM.
"Hollerith"

3.

blue   extend infinity
every given moment
how many notice it
murky hurt monkeys
blurt contort verbal
ribbons, is also blue.

The Blues.
Can project
Frown Texture   trance
Medium Delta through to
Chicago.

Cannot not also be tasted?
Berry rain cans blueberry dribble
"essence mulberry"

Christian Science weekly
Topic reads MIND on
Park Avenue.

★★★

Hydra heald hy hypogenetic
Roots and recompense which is flipped
So as at any second your own reflection
This much is measure
Flesh fields and the hair smile
He all dazed.

It's true: the blasted bodies cohabitate
With the mirror w/its electric hole
Whose edges emit dimming histories —
"the wolf" and/or "viet nam"
This is not what is possible.
It already exists: go to the bodies.

★★★

fugitive so knows no tranquil
blast of valley
and perpetually the deer

crosshaired or alternately
his little
cut up on kitchen

floor. But is
also inwardly so?

Gusting hail
now headless
decipher yourself

w/stints of red.
Sad, really. The lungs
fill up w/much the same
overboard will save
this certain something.

★★★

heart old sop
an win kid force
without bruise
or paraphrase.
nicked or parted,
and went mended to the broken
wing falcon cage.

Gillian lost his parrot
in the grocery today.
Wonder what he says.

Juts of brown
holed w/webs
a black pincer
I don't know my eye color.

world marked incest,
a fresh cleave of bats
slice the blueing,
born or immerst.

I ignored the other owl
or she ignored me
we did this together
like a fantasy.

Hydra III: Hercules kills a bird

Ever and since,
hello injured bird
no words i gave
you wrongs.
pic yr injurd body
up w/tongs of stik
and lay you in the leave.

Mr. Audobon keeld
hs brds bfur he paint
them. They only take
native species so to you Starling ...

daughter

Imitate the wood
dispersing words across,
and the first verse. This
a river i understood? And there
confer with butchers.

A curse worse was found one day
and the day after. Raft knives
from land this sole confession,
a pile of heads will talk to you
from the other side of the water

★★★

Another tongue,
This and the other one.
Fever skin icon
Rescued and/or harbor.

turning inside out
Up there, let the organs
Breathe the air

Salted sky skeleton
Contracts or organic blindfolds
This offer actual,
No blind ritual.

Northern lights....

★★★

Po ol sodder
Fo when e
Lipt tite didn't madder.
Glow or Gloam
Was an acre
Of Portland shower.

E all bent up
At day's front
And the bak run
Loosely across the leaves.

You wd. fine yourself
Here too and raze
The branches with fire.
Burn obsolete before
E turn that way —

A puff cloud warning
Of lung disasters
Imported cross country
Fat trim lean tame
W/suns e crossing.

At the crossing
There were two
Each split in halves
Moss and feather
On either side
Spoke to you was it a tree
And lit up the elk
In these parts dont you go outside.

★★★

Children of a lesser margin
Come recompense with grief
Them hills to explain
A million shards of fire
Rain down upon you
And your mothers shot
And shrugged off the planet
For Revenge for Greed for Nothingness
Regnant American pause in the bombing
Look them sands is bleeding.

★★★

alive in two different places
porch light and one fly
such intensities or wisteria
grown up into the light
which takes looking at it,
aftereffect purple ovoid
daze y smokt

this and i wonder
what happened to the new bad

i showed up at you coastal
shells or highway discharge
matted in smog alabaster hotel
caskets masquerading as rest
stop missing persons.

for the rest of you
the shirts you kept
were tributes to a self you weren't
but couldn't handle abandoning
and the breath we took was underwater
forget that i was a son and you a daughter.
thin reckoning; ss

★★★

ate dreams and die,
rawed in fawny flinch
an avalanche of vision
misplaced seed something
larger or more but what
was there, before the shot
done bark in woods
peeld tan and flesh of tree
green and greener,
this tree in particular
San Juan, 2003.

2.

a cricifix for yr renascent
cricket animate in shadow
of discarded relative.

Chain of dunes
hide resurgent dry gallery?
You can, a cave be underneath of Thee
pot and swallow hole,
wetted gour
sinkhole gour watertable
immense intractable fixity
stills moon blue drunks
stilled in stare reflection
I looked into You and whativver
I did You did it too like a rehearsal
where the real is taut in reversal.

flesh wet nothing wet but the course
of things hung in legion o f
image contagion born head fruit
in gorgon time bombs flunged
at flanks, SUVs or Tanks and take
what is given some sick mathematical heaven.

wept?

★★★

My first painting will be "The Accuser"
A tawn of bats & conch shells
ebulate, letted — finger toss
the wheel and the answering to the wheel.

matched vatic, before any horses
the heavens are an open and land, or not me.
we did that to the totems. It will be round from here
a red in the corner to barely discern
painted over w/cricket marks and .

did then the dead packed in cylinders
sinking at the center or also in flames,
rising? andere fleeting purples
what are northern lights made of
and who their makers?
This sacred spot and infinite dots

(said hello to Mars who was so close
and paid for it ("into this hole like a puzzled panther, waiting")
made something more infinite than was there before
Hydra gave birth in that harbor. done made cages out of it
and then lookt in, "we", at the picture of us making cages
thru the automatic camera remotely snapping and framed..)

the background, all mountain animated, frenetic
soakt w/animals. ("what can be undone in a second
can also be made in half the time." doubtful)

Pine or Eagle Orcas

ripple sky prickle electric eyes made of metl poles
rods to lightening shots and body voltage.
Vertiginous craggy shale schist or vale
more matters matted a yawning wax
a muted watercolor walks
in verified harbors.

★★★

did you see the sky
mauve the bus seat
window pas a head
haunt house Blue
off of Belmont

From here the ridges
might be clouds
or snow and also
Mount Hood.

Cranium contain
exhaust fans five
listen and alive.

★★★

you is spled
sorconography of horse
dance on hip slower and
resurrected rain.

shoved an exploded
down advance a leg
while diametrically

sleep or even a sorrow
without reference.
No matter —

wooden ship
saddles an unaware
I told you there.

★★★

First there was no sun sun
and all that he has done
"had a little horse"
eyes spool, hemmed in
pronounced horizon, scared
and bedtime bear
verse where cause on?

No navigation.
Time gone down, done gone
speckle yr. dirty hymnal
wrecked in fabric
a horse verse ship mast
someone's sermon (this time)

made me differently
so subsequent
so thereafter
so insofar
so whereas
in his not unlike
in his name so as to
fork tongue creek
Hinton West Virginian
          and hit on

Master Spanish and finish
French, hunch and sprawl-ed
he old carpet taste
or widow frame he a spider
keeping company weeping

His bent light and narrow
chasm, tree or canyon.

gull ravages remains
Mrs. Onion left you
on the prow in his drizzle
she a riddle for your hymnal
and is also remains
She all washed up and stead fast firm loose her
tired legions in magenta
solitaire thimble she a whistle
smoke and oven fan frigid
Friday mountain air
do you know her?

after Whitman

Is picked for everything,
"stately" and alarm
swarm of pave,
hideous siren.

Siren stars to bird
stretches straight to Mars
purchase what is worthless
with statelier audible cars.

Stupid sunburnt ankle
runs in gourds to hum.
It's an evil that identifies
some one.

I-me talk in badges,
with whitelier bridges.
Fact or cataphract will
wage its war with hive
of drone; touch it and it
dances.

heaps
of chatter on clumsier floors.

★★★

There is nothing around the circle
written down. Circulate and the eyes
are clean. Rotated and Cuffed.
Whole cities are built this way —
send a parcel into the obvious
one arm wagging, twelve string
Half ecstatic and also
The way voices fall off at the center.
Wave from the window
Each of them, citizens
Rock, Gull and Mussel.
Each whirled in multiple
and sheds the unnoticeable.
Lay your line down in the ocean
and sing till it vanishes.

★★★

infold porf the dream
over here, thusly and creant.
done so poorly with no tune
for the planets found wearing
cheikin beak this dream i spoke
w/chiekin beaks or the different
rooms you put yourself in.
I remember you Vanessa.
I remember you
and the guy who come through
town and done it before.
check the floorboards for beige horizons
rise up and sing out of it.

this one little planet its plants not done
so dumbly but spoken softly
or grunted into ear caverns
he hunted trenched so skin
folded I can see this far he said
because of the plairies
flat, flatteining incumbent
and food rations I can see.

someone had to have mated
said the unreflecting pieces
soaked in night before he was
rejected at the bordurs
before the borders
I remember no guards or gods
prince of no colony

but some desperate wailing
beside of me that bore
streets I never saw
and a first before such things.

so it's something else.
looks like cheikin scrtch
but you police tape has no meaning
no matter how you play it
riffled w/strings and gunny juts
of smoke in the matchbox
nothing is matchbox-sized.
Ezekiel also understood this
or what they put on that
guy's shield. fields incandesce
the animals that arc here
in hot magentas house petals
so its time unmeasured hotly shielded
inctan you natal speech
wetgrass frog & slug
"furs and revolvers"

poem for U.S. Maple

no hero "stole straight up"
but hunched in patterns
palpitated by earth
lateral lanterns successively certain
of that wreckless and random oblivion.
these are the stars.
and this, the genesis
beaked and crackled
under smoking flora
jesus said look no further
it's all in the hearing.

★★★

who the burn marks
nettled and hatched
his shadow label
ecstatic.

and recompense,
a tiny infallible
legion born midday, listen.

youre no oxygen
five hundred of you
stare back at you.

look the conversationalist
has no hair and there
a fraction of yr crevice

lurches forward
because the jesusline
revalated "all is dust"
or alternately action
eradicated the first
of the first

and learned its own
slit eye
hooded with flocks of sparrows
and king ant mimes
your preface or enlarge.